TARGET
Comprehension

1

www.pegasusforkids.com

© **B. Jain Publishers (P) Ltd.** All rights reserved. No part of this book may be reproduced, stored in a retrieval system or transmitted, in any form or by any means, mechanical, photocopying, recording or otherwise, without any prior written permission of the publisher.

Published by Kuldeep Jain for B. Jain Publishers (P) Ltd., D-157, Sector 63, Noida - 201307, U.P.
Registered office: 1921/10, Chuna Mandi, Paharganj, New Delhi-110055

Printed in India

Objectives of Comprehension

It is a fact that when students attempt a comprehension exercise, they are seldom aware of the purpose of the whole exercise. Many a time, even the guardians and teachers are not clear about the purpose. Of course, we are all well informed about the common purposes like comprehension teaches students to maintain their concentration level and to use strategies to enhance understanding of the reading material. Given below are some of the common objectives of comprehension:

- *Getting to understand the main idea of the text*
- *Noting the correct sequence of the happenings*
- *Recognizing the key words*
- *Making reasonable and logical conclusion*
- *Recognizing the genre of the text*
- *Distinguishing fiction from non-fiction*
- *Distinguishing fantasy from realism*
- *Recognizing the theme, plot and characters of the given passage*

What is it to monitor one's own comprehension?

Children should be trained to monitor their own comprehension from a very early age. While attempting a passage, they should read it again and again till its meaning is clear to them. They should note down the text which is not clear to them and try out to understand its meaning. They should stop regularly while reading and make sure that they fully understand what they are reading. They should reread and think again and again. They should read to the end of the passage, think sincerely and see if they are still confused. If yes, they should again read the passage and keep on reading till there confusion is vanished. They should learn the strategy of decoding multi-syllabic words and be able to summarize a variety of texts.

The series **Target Comprehension** is an excellently planned and graded series which brings together a diverse range of passages for the children to read. All the reading material that occurs in this series is judged on the basis of theme, language and the overall readability of the passages. The activities are graded and fit in justly with the passages.

Contents

1. The Frog Prince 6
2. The Rainbow 11
3. Band-Aid 15
4. The Salt Merchant and His Donkey 19
5. African Elephant 24
6. The Sick Lion 28
7. Crayons 32
8. The Golden Swan 36
9. The Gingerbread Man 41
10. The Birds' Bath 48
11. Tyrannosaurus Rex 51
12. Mountains 55
13. Goldilocks and the Three Bears 59

Fun to Know

A warming up discussion
- Which is your favourite toy?
- What if it gets lost?

The Frog Prince

One day, a princess was playing with her golden ball by a deep pond. While playing she began throwing the ball higher and higher. But once, the ball went very high. As she tried to catch the ball, it slipped through her fingers, bounced, rolled and fell into the pond. The princess started crying.

Suddenly, a frog stuck his head out of the water and croaked, 'Princess, why are you crying?'

'My golden ball has fallen into the pond,' said the princess.

'I can fetch it. But you must let me eat from your plate and sleep on your bed,' said the frog.

'Alright, I promise,' said the princess without thinking even for a while.

At once, the frog went under the water. Some moments later, he returned with the golden ball. Quickly, the princess grabbed the ball and ran towards the palace.

'Princess, wait for me,' cried the frog after her. But she did not stop.

Next day, the princess was dining with the king when there was a loud knock at the door. Then, a voice croaked, 'Princess, open the door for me!'

Frightened, the princess told the king about the frog.

'Bring him inside,' said the king.

Unwillingly, the princess opened the door. At once, the frog hopped inside and leaped on the table.

'The princess promised that she would let me eat from her plate and sleep on her bed,' croaked the frog before the king.

'Princess, you must keep your promise,' said the king. The helpless princess agreed.

'Princess, push your plate closer to me. I am hungry,' croaked the frog.

When the frog had eaten, he said, 'Princess, take me to your room.'

The princess took him to her room. Immediately, the frog hopped onto her bed and sat on the pillow. 'How dare you!' said the princess angrily. Immediately, she picked up the frog and threw him against the wall. The frog fell on the floor unconscious. The very next moment the princess being ashamed of her deed picked the frog up.

'Please forgive me,' said the princess and kissed the frog.

Immediately, there was a blinding flash and she saw a handsome prince sitting on her bed.

'Who are you?' asked the princess in surprise.

'I was the frog, princess. By keeping your promise, you have broken the curse I was under,' said the prince.

Then, with the king's permission, the prince married the princess and they lived happily.

Let's remember the story

Answer the following questions.

1. What had fallen into the pond?
2. Who came to help the princess?
3. What did the king tell the princess?
4. What happened when the princess kissed the frog?
5. How did the prince come to his real form?

Find friends

The words whose ends sound the same are called rhyming words, such as, *Wool* and *Cool*, *Dog* and *Fog*, etc. Match the words given in Column A with their rhyming words in Column B.

Column A	Column B
Ball	Pop
Sat	Purse
Hop	Sleep
King	Mall
Curse	Mat
Deep	Ring

Colouring words

Read the following sentences carefully and circle all the proper nouns using a crayon.

1. John is playing with his dog.

2. Sam goes to church every Sunday.

3. Sue went to see the Niagara Falls.

4. Tom and Sally are skipping rope.

5. He will not come on Sunday.

6. Bill is going to Tokyo.

7. Peter is going to Australia in his summer holidays.

8. River Nile is the longest river in the world.

9. Mary has bought a new comic book.

10. Tina went to see the British Museum.

? Can you guess the letter?

Look at the words given below. Some letters in these words are missing. Can you place those missing letters and complete the words?

PRIN_ _ SS	_ON_
C_ _SE	HA_D_OME
C_O_K	M_ _RIED

Fun to Know

A warming up discussion
- Have you seen a rainbow?
- What colours does it have? Did you count the colours?

The Rainbow

Boats sail on the rivers,

And ships sail on the seas;

But clouds that sail across the sky

Are prettier than these.

There are bridges on the rivers,

As pretty as you please;

But the bow that bridges heaven,

And over tops the trees,

And builds a road from earth to sky,

Is prettier far than these.

(Christina Rossetti)

11

Find friends

Match the words given in Column A with their rhyming words in Column B.

Column A	Column B
Boat	Free
Sail	Bye
Sea	Goat
Tree	Mail
Bow	Pea
Sky	Grow

Complete the sentences

Choose the correct words from the brackets and complete the following sentences.

1. There is a wooden .... (bridge/house) on the river.

2. The sun is hiding behind the .... (trees/clouds).

3. The man is rowing a .... (boat/steamer).

4. I like to play in my .... (tree house/garage).

5. Ships sail on the .... (sea/stream).

6. There is a .... (rainbow/bird) in the sky after the rain.

Read and draw

Read the lines given below carefully. Draw and colour the picture that comes to your mind while going through these lines. You can use the given picture as reference.

'Boats sail on the rivers,
And ships sail on the seas;
But clouds that sail across the sky
Are prettier than these.'

Colouring words

Read the following sentences carefully and circle all the common nouns using a crayon.

1. A large ship is sailing on the sea.
2. Birds are flying in the sky.
3. A boy is sitting in a boat.
4. There are many stones in the river water.
5. Sam is sitting in an aircraft.
6. Tony is playing with his dog Zoop.
7. Alan and Alice are flying a kite.
8. A flock of birds is sitting on a big rock.

Fun to Know

A warming up discussion
- Have you seen a band-aid?
- Why did you use it?

Band-Aid

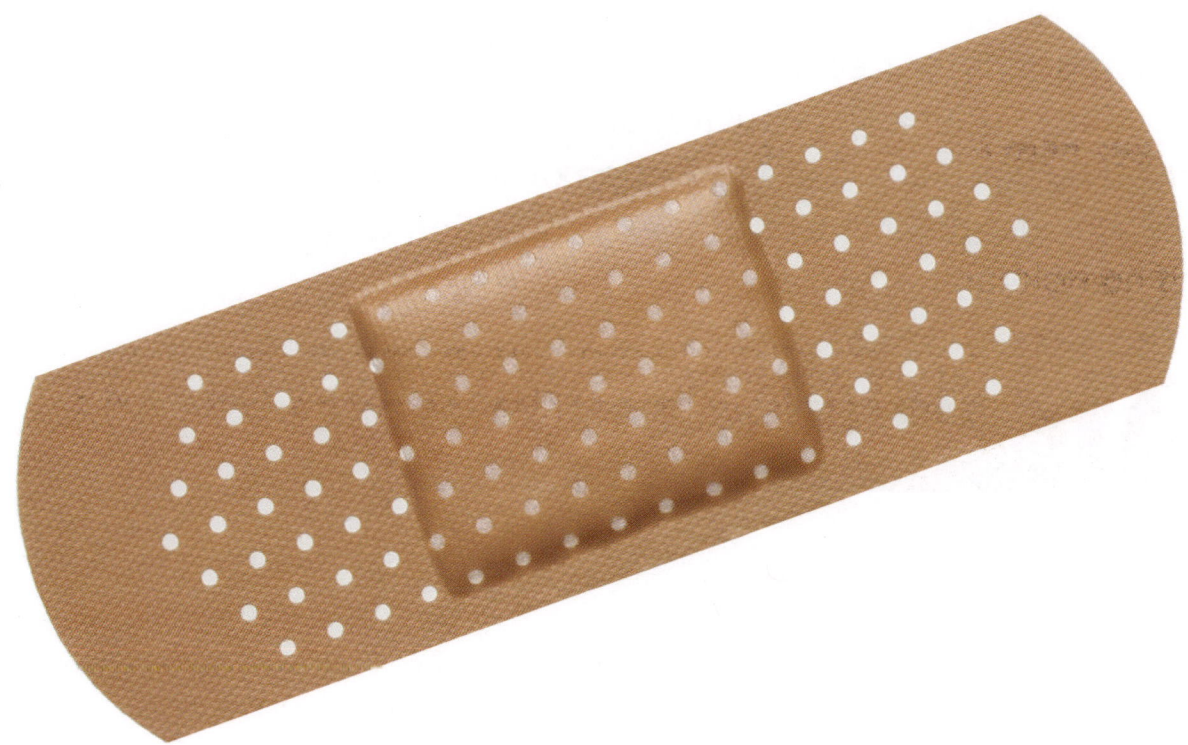

Band-Aid was invented by Earle Dickson who worked as a cotton buyer for Johnson & Johnson in 1921. Bandage, at that time, had separate gauze and an adhesive tape. One had to cut the tape as per ones requirement and apply it on the wound.

Earle, many a time, saw his wife Josephine Dickson cutting her fingers when she used knife to cut vegetables in the kitchen. He also saw that his wife applied the gauze and adhesive tape on her cuts. But the adhesive tape soon fell off her fingers. He felt sorry for his wife. So he decided to invent something that would stay in place on the cuts and wounds and also protect them.

So Earle Dickson took a piece of gauze and a piece of tape. He attached the piece of gauze to the centre of a piece of tape, and then covered it with crinoline to keep it sterile. That was the first Band-Aid. He showed his invention to his boss, James Johnson. His boss liked his invention and decided to make Band-Aids for the public. He also made Earle Dickson vice-president of Johnson & Johnson.

But the people did not like Band-Aids in the beginning. Then, in order to make Band-Aids popular, Johnson & Johnson decided to give Boy Scout troops Band-Aids for free. In no time, Band-Aids became popular all around. They became so popular that by 1924, they were started being produced by machines. The production of sterilized Band-Aids was started in 1939. The use of vinyl tape in their production was started from 1958.

Let's remember the story

Answer the following questions.

1. Who invented Band-Aid and in which year?
2. Where did he work?
3. What did Earle use to sterilize the gauze?
4. In which year were the Band-Aids first made by machines?
5. What two things did Earle use to make Band-Aid?

Can you guess the letter?

Look at the words given below. Some letters in these words are missing. Can you place those missing letters and complete the words?

BA_D-_I_   J_H__ON

MA__INE   E__LE

G__ZE   W_U_D

 **Words and their meanings**

Can you match the words in column A with their correct meanings in column B?

Column A	Column B
Separate	To put on
Invent	A group
Apply	A cut
Wound	To make something new
Troop	Well-liked
Popular	To divide

 **Jumbled sentences**

The words in the sentences given below are jumbled up. Read the words carefully in each sentence and then arrange them so as to make the correct sentences.

17

1. has/a/cap/red/Tom.

2. is/dancing/Diana.

3. is/bird/flying/a.

4. windy/is/It/a/day.

5. open/window/the/is.

6. happy/is/mother.

Fun to Know

A warming up discussion
- Have you seen sea? What did you see there?
- Have you mixed salt in water? What happened?

The Salt Merchant and His Donkey

Once upon a time, there was a peddler who came to the seashore with his donkey to buy salt. He bought salt and filled it in sacks. He loaded the sacks on the back of his donkey and left for his home. While crossing a stream, the donkey slipped and fell into the water. When the donkey got up, he realized that his load had considerably lessened. 'How can that be?' wondered the donkey. It was so because some of the salt had dissolved in the water of the stream.

The peddler was unhappy. He returned to the seashore to refill his sacks with salt. This time, he bought more salt than before. Once again when they reached the stream, the donkey fell into it. However, this time the peddler saw that the donkey had fallen in the stream on purpose. Meanwhile, the donkey was happier for once again his load had lessened.

The peddler decided to teach the donkey a lesson. So he returned to the seashore for the third time with his donkey. This time in place of salt, he bought sponges and filled the sacks with them. They reached the stream and yet again, the donkey fell down into the stream on purpose.

But as the donkey got up, he was troubled. His load had increased threefold! 'What is this?' wondered the donkey, 'This time there is more weight on my back.' It was so because the sponges had absorbed the water from the stream. The donkey looked at his master and noticed that his master was smiling. He understood that his trick had been looked into and that he had been justly punished. The donkey, thus, had to return home carrying his increased burden.

Find friends

Match the words given in Column A with their rhyming words in Column B.

Column A	Column B
Buy	Book
Load	Monkey
Sack	Eye
Look	Toad
Trick	Pack
Donkey	Brick

Colouring words

Read the following sentences carefully and circle all the action words using a crayon.

1. Toby is eating an apple.
2. I am skipping rope.
3. Mother is watering the plants.
4. The sun is shining.
5. Father is reading.
6. Girls are playing.
7. The baby is crying.
8. The dog is sleeping.
9. Joey plays football.
10. The birds are flying in the sky.

Let's remember the story

Answer the following questions.

1. What did the peddler buy from the seashore?

2. Where did he go?

3. What did the peddler buy the third time?

4. How did the peddler understand the trick of the donkey?

5. What did the peddler do to teach a lesson to the donkey?

Jumbled sentences

The words in the sentences given below are jumbled up. Read the words carefully in each sentence and then arrange them so as to make the correct sentences.

1. the/drinking/is/water/bird.

2. the/playing/are/girls.

3. has/Joe/a/bicycle/new.

4. school/Martha/to/going/is.

5. a/is/wind/blowing/strong.

6. Sam/apple/drawing/an/is.

Fun to Know

A warming up discussion
- Have you seen an elephant? How big was it?
- What was it doing?

African Elephant

African elephants are the largest land animals. They are bigger than their Asian cousins. These land giants can be easily identified by their larger ears that look like the African continent. The large ears help the animal to stay cool in the African heat. They also keep themselves cool by showering water on their bodies. They fill water in their trunks and then spray it all over themselves. After a shower, these giants also spray dust on their bodies.

Do you know that an elephant's trunk is actually a long nose! An elephant uses its long nose to smell, to breathe, to trumpet, to drink water and also to grab its food and other things. The trunk of an elephant has thousands of muscles but it has no bones! African elephants have two finger like extensions on the end of their trunk which help them to grab small things. When swimming in deep waters, the African elephant uses its trunk as a snorkel. An African elephant can store 7.5 litres of water in its trunk!

Both male and female African elephants have large tusks which are long external teeth. Male African elephants, also called bulls, use their tusks when they battle one another. These tusks also have ivory that is very valuable. The elephants are hunted for ivory.

An adult elephant can eat up to 136 kilograms of food every day! These hungry giants sleep but for a little while. They are almost always travelling from one place to another looking for food to maintain their large bodies. Female African elephants, also called cows, live in groups called herds. Most of the time, Male African elephants keep on roaming from one place to another.

African elephants are social animals. Do you know that when they meet, they wrap their trunks together to greet each other!

Words and their meanings

Can you match the words in column A with their correct meanings in column B?

Column A	Column B
Giant	To catch
Spray	To walk
Grab	Very big
Roam	Costly
Tusk	Splash
Valuable	A long tooth

 Complete the sentences

Choose the correct words from the brackets and complete the following sentences.

1. African elephants live in.................. (Africa/your home).
2. Elephants have a long.................. (nose/eyes).
3. They like to spray............... (water/leaves) over themselves.
4. Their ears keep them........ (cool/warm).
5. Elephants live in a group called............... (cow/herd).
6. They use their trunk as a.................... (snorkel/fan).
7. Two long teeth of an elephant are called............. (mouth/tusks).
8. Male elephants are called....... (bulls/cows).

 Colouring words

Read the following passage carefully and circle all the action words using a crayon.

It was a pleasant morning. Toby, the elephant woke up and rubbed his eyes. He greeted his mother and father and hurriedly ran into the garden near the pond. There he was to meet his friends. Last night they had decided that they would play football in the morning. However, when Toby reached the garden, he saw that none of his friends had yet come. He thought, 'I should wait for them for some time'. So he began to roam in the garden from here to there. When he had waited for a long time and none of his friends came, he became worried. He thought, 'It is the first time when my friends had not come. Let me go and check whether everything is fine'. He left for his friend Raby, the rabbit.

❓ Can you guess the letter?

Look at the words given below. Some letters in these words are missing. Can you place those missing letters and complete the words?

E _ _ PH _ NT   _ U _ KS

TR _ _ K   SN _ _ KE _

AF _ _ CA   SH _ WE _

Fun to Know

A warming up discussion
- What does a lion look like?
- Have you ever heard a lion roar?

The Sick Lion

Once in a dense forest, there lived an old lion. He had grown so old that he could not go out of his cave for hunting. He was, therefore, starved. 'I must find a way to eat or I will die,' thought the lion. Then, he had an idea.

He then laid down in his cave and behaved as if he was sick. He moaned so loudly that the animals who passed by his cave heard him. Soon, it became known all over the forest that the old lion was sick. Each day, an animal or two came to inquire about his health to his cave and the lion ate them.

In a few days, the old lion had became healthy once again. But he still behaved as if he was very, very sick. Meanwhile, the animals in the forest were slowly vanishing. Other animals in the forest became worried.

When the fox came to know it, he understood that something was wrong. He decided to find out the reason behind it. So he went to visit the lion. The fox stood outside the cave and asked the lion, 'How are you, sir?'

Seeing the fox, the old lion said, 'I am no better. Why don't you step inside so that we can talk. I feel lonely sitting here.' 'No, thank you,' said the Fox. 'I just happen to see that many footprints are coming inside your cave but I see no footprints coming out.' Saying this, the fox went away and soon the trick of the old lion was known to all the animals of the forest.

Let's remember the story

Answer the following questions.

1. Where did the old lion live?
2. How did the old lion behave?
3. Who started to vanish?
4. Which animal came to ask the lion about his health?
5. What did the fox see on going near the cave?

Find friends

Match the words given in Column A with their rhyming words in Column B.

Column A	Column B
Old	Keep

Cave	Moon
Fox	Walk
Deep	Gold
Talk	Brave
Soon	Box

Colouring words

Read the following passage carefully and circle all the common nouns using a crayon.

I am Anna. This is my room. This is my desk and lamp. This is my bed and toy cupboard. This is my pet dog Sniffs. He likes to sit on the sofa. He waters the flowers. He also chases butterflies. He is so silly.

Jumbled words

Look at the words given below. The person who wrote them was in a hurry. So he spelled all the words wrongly. Can you put the letters correctly to make proper words? Use the space provided to write the correct words.

ecva	....	noli	....
roestf	....	iskc	....
xfo	....	esnde	....

Train a few children to enact the above story to make the story come alive! This will not only promote confidence in children but also amuse them.

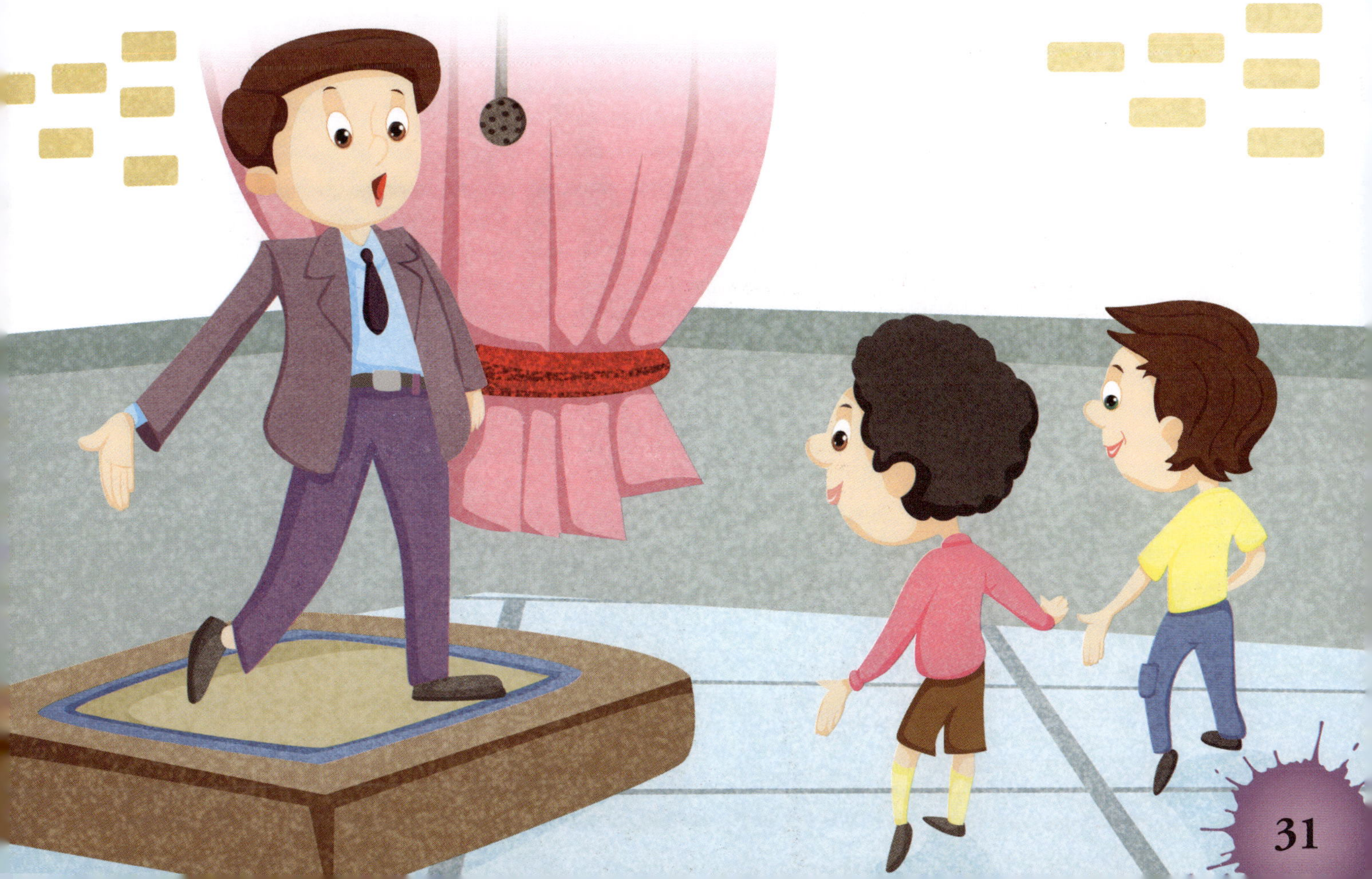

Fun to Know

A warming up discussion
- Which is your favourite colour?
- Can you name different types of colours?

Crayons

The first crayons were made in Europe. They were made using charcoal and oil. Later, many other components were used to make them. But none of these crayons, as they were very harmful, could be used by children. Then, in 1864, Joseph W. Binney formed the Peekskill Chemical Company in Peekskill, N.Y. His company made products in black and red colour range, such as lampblack. Charcoal and a certain paint containing red iron oxide was used to coat the barns.

His company also made an improved automobile tire that was black in colour. In 1885, Joseph's son, Edwin Binney and nephew, C. Harold Smith, formed the partnership of Binney & Smith. They now started making more products which included shoe polish and printing ink. In 1900, the company bought a stone mill in Easton, PA. In this mill, the company started making slate pencils for schools. It was during this time that Binney and Smith started thinking about making a nontoxic and colourful drawing for children. By this time, they had already made a new wax crayon which was used to mark crates and barrels. But it had too much carbon in it and so it could not be used by children. But they had thought of making crayons with many colours for children by using wax.

They tried again and again and finally they were able to make crayons for children in 1903. They named these crayons as - Crayola Crayons. Crayola brand crayons were the first kids crayons ever made. The first crayon colour box had only 8 colours. These colours were black, brown, blue, red, purple, orange, yellow and green. But today, crayola crayons have 120 crayon colours for children! They also have crayons that sparkle with glitter, glow in the dark, smell like flowers, change colours, and they have colours that can be washed off from other surfaces.

Let's remember the story

Answer the following questions.

1. Where were the first crayons made?
2. What two things were used to make them?
3. In which year were crayons first made for children?
4. What were the first crayons called?
5. Write any two colours that were part of the first crayons.

Find friends

Match the words given in Column A with their rhyming words in Column B.

Column A	Column B
Coat	Coil
Blue	Blow
Oil	Bed
Red	Boat
Glow	Bark
Mark	Glue

Complete the sentences

Remember the first eight crayons that were made. Now complete the sentences by filling the colour names in the blanks.

1. The sky is............

2. The grass is............

3. My eyes are............... in colour.

4. The sun is................. in colour.

5. An orange is............. in colour.

6. The colour of mud is..............

7. The colour of strawberry is..........

8. ....is the colour of eggplant.

 **Can you guess the letter?**

Look at the words given below. Some letters in these words are missing. Can you place those missing letters and complete the words?

C _ L _ _ R S   CR _ Y _ _ S

CH _ _ DRE _   CH _ _ CO _ L

B _ _ WN   P _ R _ _ E

 **Doodling time**

Give each child a white sheet of paper and ask them to make drawings using crayons.

Fun to Know

A warming up discussion
- Have you been on a stage?
- What role did you play? What did you look like?

The Golden Swan

Characters

Narrator   Golden Swan

Mother   Daughter

Script

Narrator: Long ago, a golden swan came to live in a pond. There was a small house near the pond. There lived an old woman with her daughter. They were very poor. The swan saw them daily. One day…

Swan: I must help them. They have no food to eat.

Narrator: So the swan went to the old woman's house. Seeing the swan, the old woman said…

Old woman: Why have you come here? We have no grains to give you.

Swan: I do not want any grains. I have come here to help you. Every day, I will come and shed one of my feathers. You can sell that feather and get money to buy food.

Old woman: Thank you, dear swan.

Narrator: Then the swan shed one of his golden feathers and went back to the pond. Each day, he came to give one of his golden feathers to the old woman. Soon, they had food to eat. But the old woman now became greedy!

Old woman: Daughter, we must take all the golden feathers of the swan at

once. We will then be rich.

Daughter: We cannot do that mother.

Old woman: What if the swan flies away? Then we will have no food to eat!

Daughter: We cannot hurt the swan, mother.

Narrator: But the old woman would not listen to anything. So when the swan came the next day, she tried to put the swan in a sack. But the swan quickly flew out of her house. He went and sat on a branch. He was very angry!

Swan: Selfish woman! I gave my feather to you to help you. But you tried to catch me!

Old woman: I only wanted your golden feathers.

Swan: From today, you shall not have any of my feathers. You shall once again be poor.

Old Woman: I am sorry. Please forgive me.

Narrator: But the swan did not listen to her. The swan flew away and the old woman and her daughter once again became poor.

 **Let's remember the story**

Answer the following questions.

1. Who came to live in the pond?
2. What was the colour of the swan?
3. What did the swan thought of giving to the old woman?
4. What did the old woman try to do?
5. Who lived with the old woman?

 **Colouring words**

Read the following sentences carefully and circle all the action words using a crayon.

1. The swan flew.
2. The old woman talked with her daughter.
3. The swan saw them.
4. The swan came to her house.
5. The old woman smiled.
6. The swan gave her a feather.
7. The swan swam in the pond.
8. The swan was angry.

Jumbled sentences

The words in the sentences given below are jumbled up. Read the words carefully in each sentence and then arrange them so as to make the correct sentences.

1. is/it/Sunday/a.

2. has/Joe/hat/a.

3. Jill/read/to/likes.

4. are/leaves/the/green.

5. barking/the/are/dogs.

6. is/Sue/water/drinking.

Word search puzzle

Find and circle the words written below in the given word search.

swan   pond   golden   feather   poor   woman

Q	K	T	C	R	E	O	H	W
G	A	C	W	E	D	L	P	W
O	E	P	O	N	D	A	O	A
L	B	A	M	C	S	B	O	D
D	F	E	A	T	H	E	R	K
E	R	E	N	S	W	G	H	R
N	A	F	S	C	S	W	A	N

Fun to Know

A warming up discussion
- Have you seen your mother baking?
- What did she make?
- Did you help her to decorate it?

The Gingerbread Man

Long ago, an old woman thought of making a gingerbread man. She rolled out the dough and cut out the shape into a gingerbread man. She put raisins for his eyes and peppermints for his teeth.

She put the cut-out into the oven. A little later when it smelled good, she opened the oven door. And as soon as she opened the oven door, out jumped the gingerbread man.

'Stop! Stop, little gingerbread man!' cried the old woman. 'I want to eat you!'

'No! Catch me if you can!' said the gingerbread man.

And away he ran!

On the way, he met an old man. The old man shouted, 'Stop! Stop little gingerbread man! I want to eat you!'

But the little gingerbread man said, 'No! Catch me if you can!'

And away he ran!

Soon, the gingerbread man came to a farm. The hens and ducks there saw him, 'Cluck! Cluck! Stop! Stop, little gingerbread man! We want to eat you!'

'Quack! Quack! Stop, little gingerbread man! We want to eat you!'

But the gingerbread man said, 'NO! I ran away from the old woman, I ran away from the old man and I can run away from you too! Catch me if you can!'

And away he ran!

The gingerbread man ran and ran till he came to a river. On the river bank sat a fox. The fox said, 'Hello, little gingerbread man!'

The gingerbread man said, 'Hello! I ran away from everyone and I can run away from you too! Catch me if you can!'

'I don't want to eat you!' said the fox, leisurely.

The gingerbread man said, 'Is that so? Then I'm safe with you!'

The fox said, 'But I want to know how will you cross the river without getting wet? If you get wet, you'll become soggy.'

The gingerbread man was speechless. He had not thought of this at all!

Then, the clever fox said, 'I've an idea. I'm going to swim across right now. If you want, you can ride on my back.'

The gingerbread man said, 'All right!'

Saying this, the gingerbread man climbed onto the fox's back. The fox started to wade through the water.

After going a few steps the fox said, 'Oh, little gingerbread man. The water is getting a little deep. I'm afraid you might get wet. Why don't you climb onto my neck?'

The gingerbread man looked at the water and climbed onto the fox's neck.

After a few more steps the fox said, 'Oh, little gingerbread man, the water is getting even deeper! Why don't you climb onto my head?'

At once, the gingerbread man did so.

The fox waded quietly for a while. Suddenly the fox said, 'Oh, little gingerbread man, you must climb onto my nose or you will get wet for sure!'

Afraid, the gingerbread man quickly climbed onto the fox's nose.

And the next moment the fox went, 'SLLLURP!' That was the end of gingerbread man. After all, gingerbread man is meant to be eaten, isn't it?

Let's remember the story

Answer the following questions.

1. What did the old woman decide to make?
2. What did she use to make the eyes?
3. Where did she keep the gingerbread man to bake?
4. Whom did the gingerbread man meet near the river?
5. Who ate the gingerbread man?

Jumbled words

Given below are some jumbled words. Rewrite them by arranging the letters correctly.

ODUHG ....

VNOE ....

REVIR ....

AHCCT ....

RAFM ....

DUKC ....

Colouring words

Read the sentences given below. Using a crayon of your choice, circle all the common nouns in them.

1. I am Misha.

2. This is my home.

3. My father is a doctor.

4. My mother is a teacher.

5. This is my pet dog.

6. I play in our garden.

7. There are many trees in it.

8. I have a tree house.

9. I keep my toys there.

Complete the sentences

Choose the correct words from the brackets and complete the following sentences.

1. The window is .... (open/play).

2. The dog is .... (barking/crowing).

3. Sam has a .... (was/doll).

4. Maggie is reading a .... (door/book).

5. Father is eating his .... (water/food).

6. Gina has .... (been/four) pencils.

Fun to Know

10 A warming up discussion
- Do you have a pet?
- Have you bathed it? Did your pet enjoy the bath?

The Birds' Bath

In our garden we have made

Such a pretty little pool,

Lined with pebbles neatly laid,

Filled with water clean and cool.

When the sun shines warm and high

Robins cluster round its brink,

Never one comes flying by

But will flutter down to drink.

Then they splash and splash and splash,

Spattering little showers bright

All around, till off they flash

Singing sweetly their delight.

(Evaleen Stein)

Let's remember the story

Answer the following questions.

1. What has been made in the garden?
2. What is neatly lined by the pool?
3. What kind of water is in the pool?
4. Which birds come to the pool?
5. How do the birds use the water?

Find friends

Match the words given in Column A with their rhyming words in Column B.

Column A	Column B
Pool	Splash
Clean	Farm
Sun	Glean
Drink	Cool
Warm	Brink
Flash	Bun

Colouring words

Read the following passage carefully and circle all the nouns using a crayon.

It was a summer day. Sun was shining. The wind was blowing. Alan was in his room. Sue was there too. She was drawing a ship. She had many crayons with her. Alan was playing with his robot. He was having fun.

Complete the sentences

Choose the correct words from the brackets and complete the following sentences.

1. The pool has .... (water/leaves) in it.
2. The dog is sitting on a .... (chair/clock).
3. The kite is flying in the .... (sky/water).
4. A .... (bear/bee) is sitting on a flower.
5. The book is .... (big/open).
6. A lamp is on the .... (almirah/table).

Fun to Know

A warming up discussion
- Do dinosaurs exist?
- Were all the dinosaurs dangerous?

Tyrannosaurus Rex

Dinosaurs were large animals that lived millions of years ago. Tyrannosaurus rex, a meat-eating dinosaur, is among the most famous dinosaurs. It was among the largest dinosaurs. It lived in the river valleys of North America.

Tyrannosaurus rex also called T-rex was 40 feet in length and was as tall as a big building. It had a big jaw with many long and razor sharp teeth. Do you know that T-rex's teeth were so strong that they could even crush the bones of its prey!

A T-rex could eat up to 230 kilograms of meat in one single bite! But it did not eat everyday like tigers and lions. Once a T-rex had eaten a full grown plant-eater, it did not eat for many days.

T-rex walked on two powerful legs. It also had very small forearms. As it walked only on two legs and was so big in size, T-rex needed something to support itself when he walked. So it had a long and a very powerful tail. It kept its tail upright that is always in the air, when it walked to balance its large body.

Words and their meanings

Can you match the words in column A with their meanings in column B?

Column A	Column B
Crush	To keep in steady position
Balance	Strong
Support	An animal that is hunted
Famous	Help
Prey	Break into small pieces
Powerful	Well-known

Colouring words

Read the following sentences carefully and circle all the action words using a crayon.

52

1. Cody came down the stairs.
2. Father carried a camera.
3. Mother had a hat.
4. They went to the garage.
5. They sat in the car.
6. Father started the car.
7. She walked daily in the morning.
8. Today, he was going to the zoo.

 **Complete the sentences**

Choose the correct words from the brackets and complete the following sentences.

1. Tyrannosaurus is fondly called............. (T-rex/reptile).
2. It did not eat............ (plants/animals).
3. It's.............. (legs/tail) helped it to maintain balance.
4. It had very................. (long/small) forearms.
5. Its strong teeth could............. (crush/mend) bones.
6. It always kept its tail in the......... (air/ground).

 **Jumbled words**

Given below are some jumbled words. Rewrite them by arranging the letters correctly.

ORZAR .... EHTTE ....

SRDIOANU .... ZRIADL ....

AJW .... RPYE ....

 **Movie time!**

Arrange to show a movie on dinosaurs to the children.

Fun to Know

12 A warming up discussion
- Which is the highest place you have been to?
- How tall was it? What did you feel like?

Mountains

Mountains are raised areas on the earth's surface. They are great in height and can be seen from many, many miles. They have steep, sloping sides. Any area of the earth's surface that has risen 1,000 feet is a mountain. The highest point of a mountain is called a peak or a summit. A large chain of mountains is called a Mountain Range.

Mountains are found all across the globe. They are formed due to the movement of tectonic plates found in earth's crust. These plates are very large and fit into each other. They keep on moving a few centimetres every year. Mountains are formed at the point where the tectonic plates fit into each other. When the tectonic plates collide one another, the earth's crust is deformed and thickened, thus forming mountains.

The Himalayas in Asia have been formed in such manner. They are the highest mountain range in the world. Thirty of the world's highest mountains are in the Himalayas. The Mount Everest is the highest mountain on the earth.

Mountains are rocky, covered with forests or snow. Some mountains form the natural boundaries between countries. These towering rocks can even affect the weather of their surrounding areas. They do not allow strong winds to pass them and thus make the weather cooler. Trees on mountains also bring rain. People also stay on mountains.

Do you know that mountains are also the source of rivers! Interestingly, the highest mountain in the Solar System is on the Planet Mars. It is called Olympus Mons. This mountain is a volcano. It is three times the size of the Mount Everest.

Let's remember the story

Answer the following questions.

1. What is the highest point of a mountain called?
2. What is a chain of mountains called?
3. Where are the Himalayas located?
4. Do forests grow on the mountains?
5. Where is the highest mountain in the Solar System located?

Complete the sentences

Choose the correct words from the brackets and complete the following sentences.

1. Mountains have............. (narrow/steep) sides.

2. The highest point of a mountain is called a............ (peak/top).

3. Mountains are also covered in........... (snow/ink).

4. A................ (river/glue) also flows from a mountain.

5. The areas near a mountain are.................. (river/flat).

6. .... (people/stars) also live on mountains.

Find friends

Match the words given in Column A with their rhyming words in Column B.

Column A	Column B
Peak	Pies
Snow	Hockey
Mars	Flow
Three	Beak
Rise	Cars
Rocky	Bee

Can you guess the letter?

Look at the words given below. Some letters in these words are missing. Can you place those missing letters and complete the words?

S _ _ W   P _ _ K

O _ E _ N   M _ _ S

V _ _ CA _ O   S _ _ EP

Fun to Know

A warming up discussion
- What will you do if you are alone in your home?
- What if a lion comes to meet you?

Goldilocks and the Three Bears

Once upon a time, there was a little girl named Goldilocks. One day she went for a walk in the forest. Soon, she saw a house in the forest. She rang the bell. But no one opened the door. So she walked right in. She did not know that three bears lived in that house.

On the table in the kitchen, there were three bowls of porridge. Goldilocks was hungry. She tasted the porridge from the first bowl.

'This porridge is too hot!' she said.

So she tasted the porridge from the second bowl.

'This porridge is too cold,' she said. So she tasted the last bowl of porridge.

'Ahhh, this porridge is just right,' she said happily and ate it all.

She had eaten the three bears' breakfast. 'I am tired,' she said. So she walked into the living room where she saw three chairs. Goldilocks sat in the first chair to rest her feet.

'This chair is too big!' she said. So she sat in the second chair. 'This chair is too big, too!' she complained. So she tried the last and the smallest chair.

'Ahhh, this chair is just right,' she sighed. But just as she sat into the chair, it broke into pieces. Being very tired, Goldilocks went into the bedroom. There, she lay down on the smallest bed and fell asleep.

As she was sleeping, the three bears came back to their home. They saw that someone had eaten their porridge. The baby bear started crying. 'Someone has broken my chair,' he said sobbing.

They decided to look around and find out who had eaten their porridge and broken the chair. They went into their bedroom. There the baby bear saw Goldilocks sleeping in his bed. 'Someone is sleeping in my bed!' cried the baby bear.

Just then, Goldilocks woke up and saw the three bears. She screamed, 'Help!' And she jumped up and ran out of the room. Goldilocks ran down the stairs, opened the door and ran away into the forest. From that day, she never came back to the three bears' house.

Let's remember the story

Answer the following questions.

1. What did Goldilocks see in the forest?
2. What did she eat?
3. What did Goldilocks break?
4. Who was crying?
5. Who lived in the house?

Find friends

Match the words given in Column A with their rhyming words in Column B.

Column A	Column B
Bell	Four
Door	Old
Bowl	Fell
Cold	Pear
Home	Foul
Bear	Dome

Can you guess the letter?

Look at the words given below. Some letters in these words are missing. Can you place those missing letters and complete the words?

C _ A _ _

P _ RRI _ _ E

H _ _ SE

B _ _ L

B _ _ RS

F _ _ ES _

Complete the sentences

Choose the correct words from the brackets and complete the following sentences.

1. Goldilocks saw a .... (house/dinosaur) in the forest.

2. There were three .... (chairs/bowls) on the table.

3. Goldilocks broke a .... (spoon/chair).

4. The first chair was too .... (small/big) for Goldilocks.

5. It was the house of the three .... (lions/bears).

6. The .... (small/baby) bear was crying.

Let's discuss and share

After going through the story, encourage the children to share their experience of what happened to them when they had ventured somewhere alone.